The Origin

The Origins of Christmas

Fact, fiction and myth

Roger Bush

Frederick Muller Limited
London

First published in Great Britain 1982 by
Frederick Muller Limited, Dataday House, Alexandra Road, London SW19 7JU

First published in Australia in 1981 by A H & A W Reed, Frenchs Forest NSW

Copyright © Roger Bush 1982

ISBN 0-584-95036-5

Set in 11/12 Times by Essay Composition, Sydney
Printed and bound by Caritas, Hong Kong

Contents

The Gospel Messages:
a transliteration

For just a few hours in the year man manages to gather a brief idea of his potential and a real meaning of his purpose; the wellspring of his very being.

God really DOES love him.

St Paul, of course, had been proclaiming the Gospel for some years before the Synoptic Gospels of Matthew and Luke were written. Paul concentrated upon the Crucifixion and the Resurrection as well as, in some of his letters, his own conversion. The first Christian writings were from his pen, and it was not until some years later that the Evangelists Matthew, Mark and Luke wrote their versions of the life of Jesus.

John came even later and his treatise is of a more theological nature. We might say that Matthew and Luke told what happened, whereas John gave his version as to why it happened and what it meant.

The Annunciation
Luke 1:26–38

In the sixth month a messenger, an angel named Gabriel, was sent from God to the city of Nazareth in Galilee to a maid named Mary, who was affianced to Joseph who belonged to the House of David. The maid, Mary, was a virgin. Gabriel came to Mary and spoke to her. 'Mary,' he said, 'you are the most favoured of women, the Lord is with you.'

Mary was afraid of the vision and wondered what the strange appearance might mean, but Gabriel continued to speak.

'Don't be afraid, you have found favour with God, your Father. Mary, you will conceive and give birth to a son, and when he is born you shall give him the name, Jesus. He will be a great man, others will call him the Son of God and ultimately he will be given the throne of his forebear, David. He will reign over the House of Jacob forever and his kingdom will be endless and far reaching.'

Mary asked Gabriel, 'How can all this happen? I am a virgin and have yet to know any man.'

Gabriel explained that the Holy Spirit would come upon her and His power would 'overshadow her' and that the Holy Child would be called 'the Son of God'.

'And what is more,' he added, 'your cousin, Elizabeth has conceived in her old age; indeed, she is in the sixth month of her pregnancy. She too will bear a son even though people have called her barren. You see, Mary, with God, nothing is impossible.'

Mary, overawed by all that had happened, looked at Gabriel and spoke again. 'Behold the handmaiden of the Lord; so be it as it is His will.' And the angel returned to God.

The Nativity
Luke 2:1–7

At about that time Caesar Augustus decreed that all the Roman world should be accounted for. It was the first census taken since Quirinius became governor of Syria. Each family was compelled by Roman law to return to their own town to be registered, so Joseph, with the heavily pregnant Mary, went from Nazareth in Galilee to Bethlehem, his home town.

It was whilst they were there that the time came for Mary to give birth to her child.

Accommodation was impossible to find and Mary gave birth in a place adjoining the town inn. She wrapped her child in swaddling clothes and laid him in a manger.

The Shepherds
Luke 2:8–20

In the fields nearby there were shepherds keeping watch over their flocks. Suddenly, an angel of the Lord appeared and they became terribly afraid.

'Don't be afraid,' said the angel, 'it's good news I bring, tidings of great joy. Do you realise that today there is born in Bethlehem, David's city, a child who is Christ the Lord, and who will be a saviour to you all?'

'Go and see,' said the angel. 'You will find him wrapped in swaddling cloths and sleeping in a manger.'

After the angel had delivered the message the whole sky seemed to light up and a great crowd of heavenly figures appeared and sang together.

'Glory to God in the Highest,
And on earth, peace among men in whom He is pleased.'

The angels disappeared and the shepherds agreed amongst themselves to go to Bethlehem, where they found the mother and child and Joseph exactly as the angel had described.

They repeated all they had heard and as they spoke, Mary listened to their words and wondered at them.

So they went back to their sheep, glorifying God and thanking him for all they had seen and heard.

The Visit of the Wise Men
Matthew 2:1–12

When Jesus was born in Bethlehem, Herod was king. Wise Men (probably astronomers) came from the East asking, 'Where is the new King of the Jews? We have followed his star all the way from the East and we have come to pay homage to him.'

Herod, having heard this, was afraid and so was his court and council. He called his chief priests and scribes to a meeting and asked what they knew about the birth of a Christ, and where and when he might be born.

These learned men quoted the scriptures to him:

'And thou, Bethlehem, Land of Judah,
Art in no wise least among the princes of Judah;
For out of thee shall come forth a Governor,
Who shall be shepherd of my people, Israel.'

The cunning Herod called the Wise Men and checked on the appearance and timing of the great star. He directed them towards Bethlehem and told them to search diligently.

'And,' he added, 'when you have found him, come and tell me, for I too would like to pay my respects and worship him.'

So the Wise Men left the palace and followed the star until it shone over the very place where Jesus lay.

They entered and when they saw Mary and her baby, they knelt and worshipped the child and then took their gifts of gold, frankincense and myrrh, and laid them by the manger.

As they slept that night, they too had a heavenly visitor who warned them of Herod's treachery; so they left secretly and used another route back to their homeland.

The Presentation at the Temple
Luke 2:21–22, 24–33

At the end of eight days, tradition was fulfilled and the baby was circumcised and given the name Jesus, just as the Angel Gabriel had told Mary.

It was to Jerusalem that they brought Jesus for the purification ceremony and also to present him to the Lord. There too, the traditional sacrifice of two turtledoves and two pigeons was made.

In Jerusalem lived Simeon, an old man, most righteous and holy, who lived for the birth of the Messiah. The Holy Spirit had touched his heart and assured him he would not die until he had seen the Lord's Christ. On this day, inspired by the Holy Spirit, he came to the Temple, and when Mary and Joseph brought the babe, Simeon took Jesus in his arms and cried out a blessing to God.

'Now I can die in peace', he cried. 'Mine eyes have seen thy salvation which thou hast prepared in the presence of all peoples; a light for the revelation of the gentiles, and for the glory of the people Israel.'

Joseph and Mary were amazed at all that was said about Jesus.

The Flight into Egypt
Matthew 2:13–15

After the purification Joseph again dreamed of an angelic visit wherein he was told of Herod's intention.

'Take the child and his mother to Egypt,' said the angel, 'Herod is about to search for the child and destroy him.'

So Joseph, in the dead of night, took Mary and Jesus to Egypt where they were to remain until they heard of Herod's death. An Old Testament prophet had said, Joseph remembered; 'Out of Egypt have I called my Son'.

The Slaughter of Innocents
Matthew 2:16

Herod soon realised that the Wise Men had tricked him and in a fit of rage he sent his troops to Bethlehem and the surrounding countryside and had all male children under two years of age killed.

The Return to Nazareth
Matthew 2:19–23

After Herod's death Joseph once again received heavenly guidance. An angel directed him to take the mother and babe back to Israel. So Joseph set forth upon the journey. However, he learned that Archelaus, a man almost as demonic as Herod, now reigned over Judea in Herod's place.

Wisely, and again under God's guidance, Joseph took the family to Nazareth in Galilee thus fulfilling the prophecy that Jesus was to be called 'a Nazarene' later in life.

In the Beginning
John 1:1–14

(Note: Luke and Matthew tell of the how and the where of the great event. John, in his first chapter, tells us what that great event means.)

From the very beginning God was determined to redeem men to himself. In fact this idea (the Word) was within his mind and purpose. After all, God had made all things, nothing that exists came into being without the hand of God. He alone is the source of life and the source of spiritual light.

The manmade darkness can never overcome the light of the Creator. He continues to shine in and through the darkness.

John the Baptist came to warn and prepare the way for God's regeneration of the light so that people would be ready to receive and believe.

So the great miracle occurred. The light came in the form of Jesus but men wouldn't receive Him. Even His own people refused him, but to those who had the spiritual awareness to recognise Him for what he was, God gave the gift of the Holy Spirit, powerful enough to make them sons of God.

They received a real rebirth of personality and spirit. No longer would those who accepted him be trammelled by mere humanity, but rather would they live by the will and spirit of God.

This 'idea', this integral 'Part of God', became flesh and lived with men, He was all grace and all truth and when we look at Him we see not only His glory, but God's love and glory as well.

The Church Calendar

The Church Calendar is divided into seasons to commemorate the special events of the Christian year.

Advent consists of the four Sundays preceding Christmas, then comes Christmas Day, followed by Christmas 1 and The Circumcision.

Epiphany follows with the Visit of the Wise Men and six succeeding Sundays

The Season of Advent

Advent 1

The text summing up the first Sunday in Advent is generally from Luke 21:27 'Then they shall see the Son of Man coming in a cloud with power and great glory'.

The message accentuates the Second Coming of Christ and the Gospel set down for the day is part of the prophecy foretelling the destruction of Jerusalem in A.D. 70. In the *Book of Common Prayer* in the Church of England, the lesson is often that of Christ's triumphal entry into Jerusalem and the cleansing of the Temple to symbolise the cleansing of the Church ready for his return.

Advent II

This too is a Sunday of preparation and the lectionary prescribes the passages relating to the ministry of John the Baptist. 'Art thou he who should come, or look we for another?' (Matthew 11:3)

Advent III
This Sunday views Jesus as John the Baptist might well have seen him. On this day we see Christ as the fulfilment of the Old Testament prophecy and God's promise realised in his coming.

Advent IV
Previously, the weekdays preceding the fourth Sunday in Advent were known as Ember Days. On the Wednesday, Friday and Saturday vigils were held by those who awaited ordination at first mass on the Sunday morning.

The Season of Christmas

Christmas and Christmas Day
Christmas Day is that special day of celebration to mark the birth of Jesus with a mass at midnight on Christmas Eve, followed by the traditional singing of carols and hymns on the day itself.

Originally, two masses or services were held on Christmas Day; the first a vigil, the second a feast of joy and thanksgiving.

Christmas 1
On this Sunday the glorious message is repeated with suitable lessons and scriptures, mainly from the Epistles.

Circumcision
Generally celebrated on 1 January and originally thought to be an attempt to prevent New Year celebrations of a pagan kind.

It was the custom in the early Church to have a second mass on this day in honour of the Virgin Mary who took her child back from the event of circumcision and comforted him at her breast.

The Season of Epiphany

The season commences with the visit of the Wise Men who seem, from earliest times, to have held a special place. As Epiphany progresses it celebrates in lesson and sermon the spiritual progress of our Lord.

Why the Twenty-Fifth of December?

Robert Louis Stevenson, with the aid of a quasi-legal document, presented his own birthday to a little girl who complained to him that she was disadvantaged because her birthday was on Christmas Day. In much the same way, but without really knowing why, the Christian Church came to celebrate Christ's birthday on 25 December.

There is absolutely no evidence that the birth took place in December at all. No historical record exists to show just when Quirinius held the census that brought the Holy Family to Bethlehem; and the weather conditions in December, as any pastoralist will agree, would not have been conducive to shepherds watching flocks on hills in the winter's snows.

This lack of certainty regarding the date of Jesus' birth was originally not important. There appears to have been little or no interest in the birthday until the time of Hippolytus, Bishop of Rome, in the first half of the 3rd century. He chose 2 January as the date, and the whole process of arriving at 25 December stems from that time. In those days 6 January was loosely recognised as Christ's spiritual birthday, but others in the early Church preferred other dates. To name a few: 20 May; 18 or 19 April; and 25 or 28 March.

Scholars offer two basic reasons for the acceptance of 25 December. The first is based on the old document referred to as the Plan of the Ages. By some unbelievable and almost fantastic calculations, the 'Beginning of the World' was dated at 25 March. Therefore, said the prophets, Christ, the Pascal Lamb, or the New Creation, as he is also called, must have been conceived on 25 March. Therefore, his birth took place on 25 December, nine months later.

The second reason is based on absolutely unsubstantiated evidence from John's Gospel, by which some early Church Fathers reasoned that John the Baptist was conceived in March; therefore Christ's conception took place in March. Thus again, 25 December.

While not nominating any particular month for the birth of John the Baptist or Jesus, the New Testament is specific in recording the states of pregnancy and conception of both Elizabeth and Mary.

At the time of the Annunciation, Luke (1:36) reminds us that Elizabeth was in her sixth month. If we accept March as the month in which Elizabeth conceived, then Mary conceived in September, thus setting the month of the Nativity as June, or maybe July — midsummer in Israel, and a much more likely time for the shepherds to be in the hills, rather than in the 'deep midwinter' as the carol says.

The truth is, of course, that the Fathers were influenced by pagan observances, though it is hard to determine exactly which ones. 25 March, the supposed date of conception, is related to the sun, as is also the Nativity. Celebrations for the rebirth of the sun had been recognised for centuries prior to the advent of Christianity, and probably for an even longer time the passing of the winter solstice had been a time of festivity and a recognition that the glorious sun was not dead, but actually returning to warm the earth and promote growth once more.

So in the midst of winter, when the first evidence of the lengthening days showed promise of an approaching spring, the festival of Saturnalia and Brumalia were celebrated. Saturnalia, a time of rejoicing and celebration, was held from 17 December to 24 December, and culminated with the feast of Brumalia on 25 December. Bonfires were lit in the fields and extra lights set in the homes to aid the lengthening daylight of the reborn sun and to show a joyous response for his generosity in returning to warm the earth and promote the harvest.

It was the birthday of the Unconquerable Sun or the 'Day of the Sun', namely Sunday, that became the Lord's day; likewise other pagan celebrations and festive occasions were taken over by the Church.

The Romans celebrated the Day of the Unconquerable Sun, 25 December, in joyous festivity, releasing prisoners and slaves, granting amnesties, and in general casting off almost every restraint. It is easy to understand why the Church took over this celebration as recognition of the birth of their 'Unconquerable Son' (of God).

Does the little girl, holding her doll by the tree on Christmas morning, know that for thousands of years, on this same day in ancient Rome, the father of the house gave his child the same customary present? In those pagan times, as part of the worship of the sun, tapers were lit and presents exchanged, and even then, the doll for the girl child was traditional.

Gradually and almost imperceptibly, 25 December came to be recognised as the birthday of Jesus. But not so in many of the Eastern Rite Churches. They chose 6 January and respected this date as the 'spiritual' birth which occurred with the 'physical' acceptance of Christ's entry into the world, or rather into the visible kingdom of God. This can be best understood when we compare it with the sacrament of baptism. A child, while no less a child of God at birth, is officially accepted into the visible kingdom of God at his baptism, and thus begins his Christian life.

Indeed, 6 January was first accepted by the Armenian Rite and celebrated for the first time in Jerusalem in A.D. 549 in just the same way as they do today.

To Christians, however, who attend church on Christmas morning, the date is not important. It is the event itself they celebrate in the now traditional fashion.

But we nearly never had Christmas on 25 December, or any other day for that matter.

Oliver Cromwell, the Lord Protector of England in 1655, and a Puritan, tried his best to eliminate the revelries, claiming them to be of pagan origin and therefore 'unacceptable to all God-fearing people and an abomination to the Church of Christ'. The Puritans took some of these beliefs to the New Americas with them, and for a time the same stringent rules applied there. However, when Charles II was restored to the throne of England in 1660, yuletide feasting soon became customary once again; and it still is.

The heathen origin of Christmas was no doubt tacitly admitted by St Augustine when he wrote: 'Do not celebrate that solemn day like the heathen on account of the sun, but on account of Him who made the sun'.

Stable or Cave?

Was it a stable or a cave in which Jesus was born? The New Testament says, simply, 'she laid him in a manger because there was no room at the inn'. So it could have been either a cavern at the rear of the inn or even an outbuilding. In Bethlehem to day the site venerated as Christ's birthplace is a cave, or grotto. While this is by no means the authentic site, its acceptance as such is attributed to St Helena, the mother of Emperor Constantine, who, after embracing Christianity in the 4th century, made a pilgrimage to the Holy Land, and as a result of a number of visions and dreams, nominated several places where events in the life of Christ supposedly took place. She had churches erected to commemorate those wondrous events. The Church of Nativity is just one example, but still Christians go there, as has the author, and worship on that spot with that special glow of wonder and joy that comes with the Advent season.

Perhaps the most memorable experience, during my visit to Bethlehem in April was the slow procession of people from all parts of the world, down the winding staircase to the grotto, all singing 'Adeste Fideles', but each in his own tongue. A sort of 'bonus' Christmas in April.

So, does it really matter if the date be true or false? It is the commemoration of the event that counts.

Were There Really Three Wise Men?

St Matthew does not specify a number, and tradition simply says 'three', for there happened to be three gifts — gold, frankincense and myrrh. Matthew neither names the Wise Men nor gives them any rank. It has been left to tradition and legend to give them names and identify their homelands. Thus we now sing about 'Three Kings of Orient'. We have also accepted names for them: Melchior, supposedly King of Nubia, a black man, the smallest of the three, who gave the Christ child gold; Balthazar, King of Chaldea, a white or brownish man, who gave frankincense; and finally, Caspar, King of Tarshish, the tallest of the three, who gave myrrh.

They are invariably depicted as arriving on camels, yet Eastern royalty in those days would no doubt have ridden either Arabian steeds or donkeys, not camels.

From those words in Matthew's Gospel describing the visit of the Wise Men or Magi has developed a whole set of legends. This was especially so in the Middle Ages.

The three Magi, Caspar, Melchior and Balthazar, became figures almost reaching the exalted ranks of the saints, and only because there were supposedly three gifts.

In 1158, in the Church of Saint Eustorgio, just outside the moat around the city of Milan, three bodies were found and these were accepted as those of the Wise Men. Just prior to 1164, the German Emperor Frederick Barbarossa captured Milan, exhumed the skeletons and had them taken to Cologne where they were enshrined as the Three Kings of New Testamental fame. From that time the shrine in Cologne Cathedral became a place of pilgrimage. Chaucer records that the 'Wife of Bath' made it a point of call on her pilgrimage to Europe.

In the Middle Ages it also became a custom for the rich, the powerful and for rulers, kings and princes to make special offerings of gold, frankincense and myrrh to their church on Epiphany (The Twelfth Day of Christmas).

Her Majesty Queen Elizabeth II, the present Queen of the Commonwealth, still follows this ancient custom in the service in the Chapel Royal, St James' Palace, London. Two gentlemen ushers make the offering on her behalf. The gift of 25 golden sovereigns is changed into the currency of the day and given to the poor; the frankincense is used later in the church itself, and the myrrh is sent to a hospital of the church's choice.

Epiphany marks the end of the Christmas season; traditionally known as 'Twelfth Night', it used to be celebrated by feasting and merrymaking.

A Twelfth Cake was baked, containing either a bean or a coin or token. Whoever drew the token became the King or Queen of the celebrations. Perhaps this is the origin of the coins and tokens in today's Christmas pudding, and is perhaps connected with the Wise Men bringing gifts.

The Flight into Egypt

Artists invariably depict the Holy Family struggling along past the pyramids, mainly to set the place, rather than as a matter of accuracy. Their most likely destination was Gaza, where the outer limits of Egypt were no longer under the control of Herod or his cohorts and so it was a place where Joseph, Mary and the babe could expect to find sanctuary. This area was then under the control of another Roman consul. The trip back to Nazareth

25

could then have been made in absolute safety down by the coast and along the floor of the Jezreel Valley.

Was there a 'special' star?

This has been a bone of contention among scientists and astronomers for centuries. Since few records were kept in those days, the whole matter is really one of speculation. Although the birth of Christ is generally taken to be the year 'one', the event might well have taken place within two or three years on either side of the prescribed date from which our calendar commences.

A comet was sighted in about 17 B.C., which is far too early, and another, supposedly heralding Nero's demise, was seen in A.D. 66 — far too late.

Chinese astronomers, the most expert in those far-off days, recorded the occasional sighting of a Nova, which, as we now know, is an explosion of gases. One such sighting was recorded some time around the turn of the millennium, and this could well have been the light seen over the shepherds' fields in Bethlehem.

Johannes Kepler, the great German astrologer, in 1603 discovered an ancient manuscript with the prediction that, when the planets of Saturn and Jupiter were in conjunction, a 'Messiah' would be born. He actually observed a recurrence of the planetary phenomenon in that year and, by calculation, discovered that those planets were in much the same position in either A.D. 6 or 7.

So there does seem almost irrefutable evidence for the bright light that attracted the Wise Men and the shepherds.

After all, the British Government sent Captain Cook more than halfway around the world to witness the eclipse of the sun, so one wonders if the Wise Men were similarly activated by their reading of ancient Sanskrit documents.

Can We Date the Event?

'And it came to pass in those days that there went out a decree from
Caesar Augustus that all the world should be taxed. . .'
(Luke 2:1–2)

The use of a census is by no means a product of the
computer age; it was practised in the earliest of times by
the Egyptians, the Greeks, and, of course, the Romans.

Its purpose then, as now, was to supply information
pertaining to the population, such as the number of men
available for military service, sources of income available
for tax, as well as the numbers of different races under
the heel of Rome. Rome needed the incomes from her
subject nations and Israel was no exception.

The census, as the Romans called it, was conducted
every fourteen years and counted not only the peoples of
Israel and Palestine, but also those of Spain, Gaul and
Egypt. Cyrenius (or Quirinius), the governor named by
Luke, was Senator P. Suplicius Quirinius and he is
mentioned in ancient Roman texts.

In A.D. 6, Quirinius was appointed legate to Syria and
with him went Caponius who became the first procurator
of Judea.

Sometime between A.D. 6 and 7 a census was
conducted, but this was not the one mentioned by Luke,
for by this time Jesus would have been either thirteen or
fourteen years old.

One might wonder whether Luke had made a mistake.
However, further records from Roman archives of that
period show that the same Quirinius had previously

served as legate to Syria in the days of Saturninus' proconsulship. He had served first in a military capacity when he led a campaign against the Homonadenses, a tribe in Asia Minor's Taurus mountain ranges, and then as governor of Syria between 10 and 7 B.C.

Thus the census of the New Testament took place about 7 B.C. and actually coincides with the astronomers' findings about the bright and strange star.

It seems, then, that both astronomer and historical evidence join hands, or rather, minds, about the date of the great event, the birth of Jesus in Bethlehem in A.D. 7.

A Modern Tale of Three Wise Men

The current fashion seems to be to re-write history to suit any specific occasion. The Bethlehem story lends itself quite well to this technique, for the Wise Men did not really come from the East at all, as we are so often told, but actually from the West.

See them, then, in a different light, travelling towards the star carrying their gifts, and bringing with them as well all the questionable benefits from a western society.

Here is Caspar, the best business brain from the West, the Managing Director and principal shareholder in Caspar Manufacturing & Retailing Incorporated, producers of consumer goods *par excellence*.

He sees unlimited opportunity in the trip. Armed with catalogues, discount lines, and tremendous ambition, he begins his journey under the star's bright light, pausing every now and again to purchase a site, to recruit staff to handle his exports and to throw the odd party to celebrate the opening of a new store.

He is particularly happy, for not only can he see the dollars rolling in, but the whole trip is tax deductible and his expense account open to all sorts of wily negotiations and shady deals.

Unfortunately, his business affairs keep him just a little too long in Damascus and he arrives in Bethlehem to miss the Holy Family, who have taken off for Egypt the day before.

Melchior more or less accompanies him. He is the military genius from the West with his stock of slightly used last-war armaments on sale at a suitable discount price. He decides that the new king might well want to establish some sort of military regime, so he comes with his bargains; a few FIIIs, rockets, and superseded atomic warheads.

The countries through which he travels also have need of some of his hardware, so he holds field days and demonstrations of his arms. His rocketry and air-to-air missiles so brighten the sky that he actually loses sight of the special star, so he promptly forgets all about the real purpose of the journey.

Not so Balthazar, of the Advertising and Public Relations firm of Balthazar, Balthazar and Balthazar, and in the terminology of the trade, 'a pretty smart cookie'.

Balthazar, or B.L. as he is known, sees the real magnitude of the event. A star, a New King, and what have you, as 'living history'. Here is a P.R. exercise he can really get his teeth into. The event has to be handled on the grand scale. This is something for posterity with a capital 'P'.

So B.L. takes along a couple of secretaries, a top-line copywriter, and a copying machine (on contra of course) and sets about producing and distributing press releases to the newsagencies in the towns through which he passes.

Good stuff, too, and popular with the local press.

So colourful and newsworthy is his material, so magnificent his project, that he detours through Egypt, Syria and Lebanon to gain extra coverage, which takes him a couple of extra months . . . So he misses the Great Event altogether.

So the poor Child never received the Wise Men's gifts after all.

History, then, is best left alone, with the Wise Men coming from the East. The West, with its commercial know-how, its military capacity, and its slick promotional skills, still seems to miss the real message and more often than not it misses the way to Bethlehem.

The Nativity Scene

Christmas, anywhere in the world, just would not be the same without the scene depicting the Holy Family — that set of figures or figurines we have come to call the crib or the creche. The Nativity scene is encountered at the altar in our church, in shop windows, at theatre entrances, in fact anywhere in the Christian world at this season.

The first such scene was devised by St Francis of Assisi in 1224 in Greccio, Italy. Seeking to impress his parishioners with the simplicity and stark reality of the humble fashion in which God became man, he presented a Nativity scene with a difference. His characters were real. Local folk from Greccio acted the parts and real animals were used — cattle, sheep with shepherds, and so on. The legend does not suggest that a real child was used in place of Jesus, but there is little doubt that this annual 'morality pantomime' taught the humble folk of Greccio, as it has taught us down through the years, the timeless message of Christmas.

Today, Nativity scenes grace the facades and windows of department stores the world over. Hardly a home or a church celebrating Christmas, is without a facsimile of St Francis' original scene, set up year after year, either near the Christmas tree, the altar or on the mantelpiece.

The remarkable feature of each of these scenes is that the characters bear a distinct resemblance to the people of the particular country celebrating Christmas. The

Japanese Christ Child is an Oriental doll, and in the Philippines the Holy Family is unquestionably Filipino. All remember, and indeed demonstrate, the universality of God's grace at Advent.

Christmas Across The World

Armenia
Where they say 'Schenorhavor Dzenount'

The Eastern Orthodox Church of this country leans towards the profundity of the religious aspect of Christmas, but this does not in anyway prevent special celebrations. Here the children mount the housetops, and from this vantage point they sing songs of rejoicing and carols of the Nativity, proclaiming the good news of Christ's birth. After they come down from the rooftop they are given their Christmas presents — a type of 'singing for one's supper' in much the same way as Little Tommy Tucker of the nursery rhyme. Whatever its origin or rewards, the children enjoy the custom.

Australia
Where they say 'Merry Christmas'

As in the USA, many, if not all, of Australia's Christmas customs are imported, but in recent years some typically Australian carols have been composed and are finding a special place in the repertoires of church choirs and carol services.

During December, 'Carols by Candlelight' services are held throughout the land, generally sponsored by Church groups and Service Clubs. They are held in local parks and shopping centres, and the children attending are given lighted candles to hold during the services.

In many homes in Australia, salads, hams and cold poultry are served for Christmas dinner, rather than the traditional hot dinners of Europe and the colder climes.

It will be interesting to see which (if any) of the customs brought to Australia by the hundreds of thousands of immigrants will become part of the national scene at Christmas time. But no matter what customs find new roots in the land down under, none will ever be as unique as the outback practice of using the Flying Doctor Radio Service to pass Christmas greetings from homestead to homestead on Christmas Day.

Belgium
Where they say 'Vrolijke Kerstmis'

In Belgium, so the children believe, Saint Nicholas (their version of Santa Claus) actually makes two visits. First, he comes to check whether the children have been good and are deserving of reward. He then departs to his workshop and returns again on Christmas Eve. In the meantime, the children place water and hay in a prominent place to attract Saint Nicholas' white horse. After all, they suggest, he too, is worthy of reward for carrying Saint Nicholas and his never-empty bag of toys so far and so late.

Then, in special places of their own choosing, by the fireplace, the bed, or under the tree, they place their baskets or their shoes for Saint Nicholas to fill with his presents for them. Rumour has it that more than one naughty child has been left a cane, rather than goodies, to remind him to behave a little better in the future.

35

Czechoslovakia

Where they say 'Vesele Vanoce'

In this country the good folk used to fast until Christmas Eve, when it was time to begin feasting and dancing in the streets. It was also time for visiting friends and relatives, and carollers roamed the streets carrying scenes of the Nativity mounted on boards. Boys dressed as the Three Kings from the Orient gave on-the-spot performances in return for sweets and cakes, like the strolling players of old.

These customs are particularly Czechoslovakian, but the Czechs share many other customs with the rest of Europe. However, the Iron Curtain has dropped and the State has forbidden Christian festivals.

Here is a copy of a memo issued in 1976 by Government House, Prague:

Because Christmas Eve falls on a Thursday, the day has been designated a Saturday for work purposes. Factories will close all day, with stores open a half-day only.

Friday, 25 December, has been designated a Sunday, with both factories and stores open all day.

Monday, 28 December, will be a Wednesday for work purposes.

Wednesday, 30 December, will be a business Friday. Saturday, 2 January, will be a Sunday, and Sunday, 3 January, will be a Monday.

Be that as it may, Christmas Day in 1976 fell on a Saturday, so maybe in Communist-dominated countries the calendar may have been changed as well!

Denmark
Where they say 'Glaedelic Jul'

Denmark celebrates in much the same way as most Scandinavian countries but with a distinctively Danish touch. Special Danish dishes are prepared, and a particular favourite is *brunekager,* a cookie or biscuit flavoured with molasses and spice.

Another lovely custom is one that demands the householder and farmer show care for birds and animals. Posts are set in the ground with sheaves bearing the best of grain. On some posts and above the doorways and windows of the houses, bread and suet are placed for their feathered friends. The greater the number of birds that come to eat these gifts, the better the ensuing harvest.

Another custom is the lighting of the *julebaal,* or bonfire, which is visible from the main room of the home where the celebrations take place.

After dinner, the parents retire to the room with the tree and the youngest child is accorded the privilege of being first to see the lighted tree and open the first present. At night, it is not Santa who comes, but the Nisse. He is a tiny little fellow about the size of an elf or a sprite. These mythological creatures bind themselves to Danish farmhouses for all time. In fact, the Nisse is the sole survivor of pre-Christmas mythology of the Danish yuletide of yesteryear.

The special charitable seals on Christmas mail now common throughout the world were introduced by Einar Holbull, a Danish postmaster, in 1903. Royal approval by Queen Louise was given in 1904, and her portrait graced the seal, which was sold for the welfare of the poor.

England and Wales
Where they say 'Merry Christmas'

Since the 19th century, it has been hard to separate Charles Dickens from the English Christmas. His story, *A Christmas Carol,* and its characters Tiny Tim, Old Scrooge and the line 'God Bless us everyone', are by now completely interwoven with the English festive season.

But there are other traditions particularly English, such as the Christmas pudding. Legend has it that some ancient king of days gone by was lost in the fog one Christmas Eve. He and his few retainers were not only thirsty, but, the story goes, pangs of hunger gnawed at their vitals. So the king and his men pooled their meagre rations of plums, flour, fruit and the like, wrapped the whole mess in a large cloth and boiled it. The result, to those hungry men, was a delicacy beyond description. Indeed, the king was so pleased, he decreed that this pudding be the special dish for his kingdom every yuletide.

England also claims the right to the very first Christmas card, but more about that in another part of this book. Another English legend is that of the Glastonbury Thorn. The thorn bush blossoms at Christmas time, and the tale goes that some time in the very early days of Christianity, Joseph of Arimathaea came to England and visited Glastonbury. He carried with him a stave from the Holy Land and during one of his rest periods he stuck the stave in the ground. It took root and grew, so he simply left it there. And they say he celebrated the first Christmas in England just by the newly growing thornbush. The bush flourished in Glastonbury for many years, until the church was burned down. But shoots of the shrub were preserved, and now it grows all over the country.

England is not without some strange old customs from the days of the Druids and other ancient or legendary groups. In Yorkshire, for example, it was once the custom for a group of boys to attend church and give the parishioners large apples from the basket they carried. In Devonshire it used to be the custom for single girls to go to the hen house on Christmas Eve and knock seven times. If a hen cackled, their future was supposedly a bit gloomy, but should a rooster crow, then without doubt they would be married before the year was out. Again, if a single girl walked backwards towards a pear tree on Christmas Day, and then walked around it three times, she would then see a vision of her future husband. Old wives' tales, of course, but then, they do make Christmas rather special, don't they?

Wales boasts the finest choral music in the world. Each year, special Eisteddfods are held during the festive season to find the best original works composed and performed especially for Christmas.

People also say that Welsh Christmas pudding is the finest in the world and will keep for years.

Finland

Where they say 'Hauskaa Joulua'

If you have always associated the sauna bath with Finland, then you will not be surprised to know that the Christmas celebrations there begin with a sauna the night before the celebrations begin.

The Christmas Eve meal is a light one, eaten at the family table, over which is suspended a manger. The floor is strewn with hay and straw as a reminder of the stable where Christ was born. After dinner the menfolk used to wrestle. After the festivities, as bedtime approached, the children slept on the straw to remind them of their Saviour's birth.

Father Christmas brings the presents during the night, and the following day, Christmas Day, is set aside for religious observance rather than as a day of festivities.

France
Where they say 'Joyeux Noel'

While France shares most of her customs with her neighbours, there are one or two that are uniquely French. The yule log has a central and special place, and the whole family take part in cutting it down and bringing it to the hearth, where it is lit on Christmas Eve. It must be large enough to burn through until the evening of New Year's Day, for if it does, there is a special blessing on the household and a sure prevention from damage by thunder and lightning.

In some communities in France, Christmas actually begins on Saint Barnabas' Day, 4 December. On this day a number of plates are placed either near the warm fireplace or on a sunny window sill. Water and wheat seed are placed on the platters, and the germination is watched with great concern. Should the wheat spring and every seed germinate with a tiny green shoot, then the promise is for a good harvest. If, however, the shoots are limp and poor, then the year's harvest will be the same.

After Midnight Mass on Christmas Eve, the children sleep, and are visited by 'Pere Noel' who bears good things for them, and on occasions, by his counterpart, 'Le Pere Fouettard', who administers 'spankings' on the bottoms of the children who have not been so well behaved.

Germany

Where they say 'Frohe Weinachten'

St Nicholas doesn't come on Christmas Eve in Germany but on the evening of 5 December. Children leave their shoes outside the door, and, provided the shoes are properly cleaned, St Nicholas leaves them full of goodies, sweets etc.

The real celebration at the family level is held on Christmas Eve. Sometime prior to that special time, mother and father close off the lounge or sitting room and decorate the tree. The rest of the family are denied entry until perhaps 7pm on Christmas Eve, when, to their surprise, the 'Angels' have dressed the tree beautifully, with some of the gossamer from their wings forming part of the decoration. A previously prepared plate of special sweets for each family member is placed under the tree. Presents are distributed when the 'oohs' and 'aahs' are over and a light meal of soup, salad and frankfurters is taken; gluehwein is generally the drink.

Later the family attend either the Midnight Mass if they are Catholic or the 11pm service if they belong to other denominations. On Christmas Day, the children, as with children everywhere, show off their presents to their friends.

Greece

Where they say 'Kala Christougena'

Greeks celebrate Christmas from Christmas Eve through to Epiphany, and besides most of the usual customs, have one or two that are decidedly their own.

A special loaf of bread is baked for Christmas. The family watch and share in its preparation, and the top of the loaf is marked with a cross, not unlike our Easter hot cross bun, and a coin is placed inside. (Remember the

41

silver coins in the Christmas pudding?) The bread is broken at a family meal, and while it is shared by the whole family, the loaf is divided into four portions. The first portion is set aside for the Mother of Jesus, the second for the home, the third for the animals of the farm, and the remainder is shared by the diners in the home. Needless to say, only tiny symbolic portions are set aside for Mary, the home and the animals. The finder of the coin, if single, will be fortunate in marriage, and if already married, enjoy good fortune in the ensuing year.

As in other parts of Europe, the Christmas log plays a part; so do some mysterious creatures called *karkantzari* — elf-like sprites who do good and happy little things about the household.

Holland
Where they say 'Zalig Kerstfeest'

In Holland, Saint Nicholas comes on 6 December and rewards the well-behaved with good things and admonishes the misbehaved. Christmas Eve and Day are times of deep religious observance.

In the rural areas of this country, it is a joy to see the fine lace and crochet work on the special hats worn by the womenfolk to Mass on Christmas Eve.

Traditionally, Santa Claus or Saint Nicholas, comes in from the sea in a ship — a custom handed down from the time when Holland was occupied by Spain. The Good Saint is attended by Black Peter, clothed in the pantaloons and garb of the days of Spain's former glory, and the strange thing is that he knows all about the bad things little children have done, and sometimes goes as far as to threaten them with 'no presents'.

Saint Nick and Black Peter are greeted by the Dutch Royal Family, and later, in almost every household, some friend or relative plays the part of Black Peter, who manages to confound the children with the knowledge he possesses of their past year's conduct.

Hungary

Where they say 'Boldog Karacsony'

In Hungary, Kris Kringle, not Santa Claus or Saint Nicholas, comes on his white horse, his grey horse, or even a grey donkey — not that it matters, so long as he arrives. The donkey, of course, is related to the donkey that bore Mary from Nazareth to Bethlehem that wonderful Christmas Eve so long ago.

Some of the magic of the Dark Ages still surrounds the yuletide season in this country. Ashes from the burned yuletide log are scattered about the roots of trees to ensure a good harvest for the coming season. At the main meal an apple is cut in two, and is supposed to indicate the health a person can expect for the ensuing year. A clearly defined star pattern of the seed-pod within the apple indicates good health, whereas a not so clearly defined star denotes bad health. Mythology and a blend of Eastern and Western cultures suggest that this custom is somehow connected with the apple of the Tree of Knowledge in Genesis, but the real origin is lost in history. Such a custom is probably very old, because the Aborgines in Australia have a similar custom. They use a cut root, rather than an apple, to determine disease and health prospects.

Ireland
Where they say 'Nodlaig Nait Cugat'

One would think that the 'Little People', so much a part of Ireland's folklore, would have found a special place in their Christmas celebrations, but this is not so. Country lads, however, have an odd custom. They build an ornate little cage on top of a pole, catch a wren and imprison it temporarily in the cage as they go from house to house, crying:

'The wren, the wren, the King of all birds,
Saint Stephen's Day was caught in a furge,
Although he is small, his family is great,
So arise, landlady, and give us a trate.'

They say this racket works quite well.

The creche or Nativity scene is the centre of every home in Ireland at Christmas, and Christmas trees are very rare indeed. However, a light shines in every window, and every door is unlatched. This is because custom suggests that the Virgin may be seeking a place to have her child, seeing there was no room at the inn on that auspicious occasion. The custom of lights in the window is supposed to have originated in Ireland.

Italy
Where they say 'Buon Natale'

Besides the wonderful celebrations held in Saint Peter's Church in Rome, where the Holy Father usually celebrates Mass, and where pilgrims come from all over the world, Italians have some customs that are peculiarly their own.

In Italy, it is the custom for children to write Christmas letters or poems to their parents and place them under the plate at the Christmas Eve meal. In the country areas, shepherds come down from the hills to sing carols, or take a special part in the evening Mass. It is also the custom to sing and sometimes pray before the carpenters' shops throughout the land as a mark of special respect to Joseph, who was also a carpenter.

Santa is replaced by Beffania, an elderly fairy who leaves gifts for children, as does Santa in other lands. But in Italy, it is always on Twelfth Night, that is, the eve of the twelfth day after Christmas, that he comes. For the good children he leaves sweets and presents, but for the naughty, dirt and stones in their stockings.

Lithuania

Where they say 'Linksmu Kalendu'

Many of Lithuania's customs are similar to those of the neighbouring Scandinavian countries, but, like most countries, one or two special customs make them just a little different.

The Christmas Eve dinner in Lithuania is the real Christmas feast. The table is spread with straw to remind the family of the humble birth of Jesus and the manger of Bethlehem. But the feast consists of twelve courses, a symbolic reminder of the twelve apostles. Here, gifts are only given to the children and the very old.

Mexico

Where they say 'Feliz Navidad'

In Mexico the family celebration on Christmas Eve takes on a somewhat competitive air. Sweets and gifts for the children are wrapped in a large paper bag and suspended from the ceiling. The children are blindfolded and each is given a turn at attempting to break the paper bag with a stick. Imagine the merriment when the bag is broken and the goodies are strewn all over the floor. Obviously, the child breaking the bag always seems to miss out, but compensation is made with a special gift awarded to him or her as a prize.

Then when the children are asleep, the giver comes. Not Santa, for the Mexicans are the descendants of the Aztecs, children of the Sun God, Huitzilopochtli. He comes in the form of a great and kindly feathered serpent, who, rather than terrifying the youngsters, is held in great affection by them.

Poland
Where they say 'Wesolych Swiat'

In Poland legend and profound religious celebrations join hands with ancient customs that are often linked with old fertility rites. For instance, the apple tree is shown a sharpened axe on Christmas Day as a reminder of the New Year. Sometimes the trunks of trees that have not borne well are whipped with birch rods and stones are hung from the branches as a symbol of humiliation.

The most important celebration is the family dinner, served on Christmas Eve. The table is set, straw spread under and about its legs as a reminder of the manger, and the family gathers at the window to watch and wait for the first star to appear before commencing the meal. An empty chair is left at the table for the expected Christ Child, who, so many early European folk-tales tell, supposedly wanders the world seeking shelter each Christmas Eve.

Not unlike the carol singers of other countries, musicians wander the streets playing Nativity hymns on violins, or other instruments.

Gifts are exchanged on Saint Nicholas' Day, 6 December, and that dear old Saint leaves gifts under the pillows of both adults and children. Then later, on New Year's Eve, gifts are left by 'guardian angels', but with a difference. Children who have been naughty find not a present under the pillow, but a switch, to remind them to behave a little better in the New Year.

Romania

Where they say 'Sarbatori Fericite'

Here the men and boys make a large star, mount it on top of a long pole and dress it with tinsel and coloured paper. Bells are attached, and the completed *Steaua* is carried from house to house as they sing, recite, and generally perform in return for gifts of sweets and cake. Occasionally, the star is illuminated with candles and bears an icon-like picture at the centre; invariably the picture is of some aspect of the Nativity. The pole, the star and all, is often referred to as the Heavenly Lantern.

Russia

Where they say 'S Rozhestvom Krvstovvm'

Apart from the Russian Orthodox Church, where the services are of a purely religious nature, and the underground Church, which offers only the prescribed Masses and services, Christmas is a forbidden festival in Russia.

Once it was that the goodly folk celebrated in other ways. Many of the Central European customs were observed in Russia, and in the old days, stockings and shoes were placed outside the door of the family home for Old Man Winter to fill with good things. Traditional presents for the young in those days were red boots for the boys and golden slippers for the girls of the family.

Sweden

Where they say 'Glad Jule'

Christmas in Sweden begins, officially, on 13 December, which is Saint Lucia's Day and is declared 'open' by the Lucia Bride. The Bride is usually represented by some young female member of the family who takes the place of the traditional Saint Lucia, who, in past times, went about carrying food and drink to the poor and hungry of her district. She wears a full-length white frock, with a very wide red sash, and on her head she wears a wreath-like crown of leaves adorned with candles. The Bride goes through the household, awakening each member of the family, in turn, serving them hot coffee and freshly baked bread or buns as breakfast fare. Sometimes she has with her the traditional 'baker's boys' who carry *Lussikattor* or Lucy-cakes. Not unlike gingerbread men, the Lucy-cakes are cat-shaped saffron buns with raisins for eyes.

Incidentally, Saint Lucia was supposed to have been martyred. She burned at the stake rather than give up her faith and marry a pagan.

In the farming areas all farm work must be completed before Christmas Eve in readiness for the *Julotta,* or Christmas Day Mass, which is held in the dark of the morning. Sleigh-loads of worshippers drive to Mass in the early morning, each sleigh lit with either a candle or a flaming torch. On arrival at the church all the torches are tossed on to a great pile of combustible material, and before a blazing bonfire the congregation sing their carols of the Nativity. Then back home to a quietly celebrated day.

When the Swedes present their gifts on Christmas Eve, they are usually accompanied by a four-lined rhyme of the giver's composition. A special dish is prepared for Christmas Eve. *Grot* is a rice dish cooked with milk and garnished with cinnamon, and buried somewhere in the 'pudding' is a single almond. The lucky lass who finds the almond, so says the tradition, will either see her prospective husband in a dream that night, or be married in the ensuing year.

Switzerland
Where they say 'Froehliche Weihnachten'

Because of the mixture of cultures in this alpine country, Christmas is celebrated in various ways. Saint Nicholas arrives on 6 December in some parts, while in others it is *Sammich-laus,* wearing a mask and dressed in furs and sporting a long white beard, who visits the houses. In some areas Father Christmas and his wife, Lucy (Saint Lucia) give out the toys on 12 or 13 December. And believe it or not, or just to add to the confusion, the Christ Child comes on Christmas Day in a sleigh drawn by six reindeer, distributing gifts to deserving children.

The children of Switzerland might be forgiven for not knowing just when Christmas really is!

Spain

Where they say 'Feliz Navidad'

For many years in Spain it was the custom to release minor offenders from prison on Christmas Eve and present special gifts to people in hospital. No one goes to bed before midnight on this night, and each person must be able to record at least one good deed performed before the end of the year. On Christmas Eve, the streets are filled with people looking for an opportunity to perform such a deed before retiring for the night.

There is no snow in this part of the world at Christmas, but a surfeit of fiesta and merrymaking commences after Midnight Mass on Christmas Eve.

Personal gifts are not exchanged until Epiphany Eve, the night of 5 January. On this night, shoes and slippers piled with straw are left on the window sills for the tired camels who have brought the gift-bearing Wise Men so far. The Kings respond by leaving gifts as a reward, and thus everyone is happy.

United States of America

Where they say 'Merry Christmas'

Christmas customs in the USA originally crossed the Atlantic with the Pilgrim Fathers. With a faith and a doctrine that found its genesis in Calvin, the celebration was deeply religiously orientated, but was invariably followed by a grand and traditional English style feast, complete with poultry and pudding. Simple home-made gifts were exchanged, for Santa Claus was as yet unknown.

The turn of the present century brought countless thousands of immigrants and with them the Christmas customs of their erstwhile homelands. Ethnic groups celebrate in much the same way as their forebears in their first year in the new homeland. In Minnesota, for example Christmas takes on a Germanic flavour, while in Pennsylvania the Dutch Americans cling, quite unknowingly, to customs and practices brought over by great-great-grandparents perhaps a hundred years before.

While the USA's oldest Christmas carol was written by an anonymous missionary for the Huon Indians in 1641, Tin Pan Alley and the film industry have given the world some of its favourite yuletide songs. 'I'm Dreaming of a White Christmas' and 'Christmas in Killarney' are two such examples. Needless to say, performers have not been backward in recording many of the popular Christmas tales.

Each year one American newspaper publishes a list of 'The Most Unusual Christmas Presents', and not so many years ago the prize for originality was presented to the manufacturer who gave the world its first mink toothbrush!

But the pudding, the cake and all the trimmings of Christmas are most certainly present, and most Americans celebrate Christmas in the traditional way.

The customs throughout Europe are similar but most groups of people have added little touches of their own which give a distinction to the celebrations.

The Norwegians give special attention to the birds and animals who find it hard to forage for food on the frozen and snow-covered ground. Mother also bakes a special bread made in thin wafers from oatmeal flour, not unlike low calorie wafer biscuits for trying to lose weight.

In the old days in the Ukraine, the faithful would precede Christmas with a forty-day fast, and end the fast with a gigantic twelve course meal.

In most emergent countries, where a Christian minority celebrates the festive season, they have accepted the customs brought from the homelands of the missionaries. For instance, the Methodist choir in the big Central Church in Fiji sing the traditional carols in Fijian but use the same tunes as their fellow Methodists in other parts of the world. In much the same way, Aboriginal children from central Australia's Lutheran Hermannsburg Mission sing their carols in German.

It is only within the last decade, since churches in places like India, Africa and the Pacific Islands have become self-governing, that new carols more suitable to the indigenous people have been composed, carols that perhaps express more clearly, for them the great message of Advent. Similarly, in countries like America, Canada and Australia, where large immigration programmes have been conducted in the post-war years, new Christmas music and carols have been composed and written to help assimilate newcomers into their environment.

But the traveller at Christmas time need have no fear of not being able to participate for whether the congregation worships in Bantu, Congolese, in Fijian or Samoan, or even that most difficult of all languages, Japanese, he will feel at home, for the sight of the crib will break the communication barrier. As long as he knows the words of the familiar old carols, he will be able to sing along with the congregation.

Christmas in Wartime

The First World War

That the spirit of Christmas invades the very soul of men is true, no matter what the country, the time or the place. The countries in this story are England and Germany — the time, Christmas Eve 1915, and the place, the bloody trenches of the Somme.

The fighting had died down, the soldiers of both sides were resting. Perhaps a few were trying to sleep and maybe one or two were writing a few brief words by flickering candlelight to a loved one in either Berlin or Birmingham. But all of them, German and English alike, were trying to keep warm in the frozen dugouts amidst a sea of mud. The barbed wire battlefield was quiet — quieter than it had been for months — and it seemed to the sentries on the firing steps that the quietness, itself, was ominous. Could it be, one Tommy wondered, the calm before the storm of another bombardment? He could almost anticipate the whine of the shells and the chatter of machine guns.

Then, gazing across at the German emplacements, he heard, almost imperceptibly at first, the sound of singing. The words were in another language, but the tune he had known from boyhood — 'Stille Nacht, Heilige Nacht'.

Hardly believing his ears, he called his comrade. 'What's going on out there?' he demanded.

'It's the Jerries — it's Christmas Eve,' the soldier replied.

And as if to confirm his diagnosis, a voice from the German trenches called across those few yards of hell,

'Merry Christmas, Tommy,' to which there was a spontaneous reply, 'Merry Christmas, Fritz'.

'It was like a miracle', one of the participants told me. 'First we waved capes on the ends of our rifles, both sides, then we stuck our heads up, one by one, both sides. It all took only a few moments, and suddenly there we were, all out in no-man's land, both sides exchanging cigarettes, sharing food, swopping cap badges, slapping each other on the back and shaking hands. We showed each other pictures and snaps of our families at home, and with the help of an old concertina, we sang 'Silent Night', 'Come All Ye Faithful', and a few other carols. Then, after about half an hour or so, we all went back to the mud and blood of our own trenches. And then, believe it or not, the next day, we were blowing each other to kingdom come.'

The Second World War

Guy Sajer, in his book *The Forgotten Soldier,* published by Harper & Row, gives a poignant description of a sixteen-year-old German soldier's most memorable Christmas on the frozen hell of the Russian Front in 1942.

'My nose, the only part of me directly exposed, began to burn with cold. I had pulled my cap down as far as I could, so that my forehead and part of my cheeks were covered. Over this I wore the helmet required for guard duty. The turned-up collar of the pullover my parents had sent me overlapped the edge of my cap at the back of my head.

'From time to time I looked at the expanse of machinery I was guarding and wondered what we would do if we had to move it all in a hurry. The engines must have reached a state of magnificent solidity!

'I had been at my post for a good hour when suddenly a silhouette appeared at the edge of the parking lot. I threw myself down into the bottom of my hole. Before extracting my hands from the depths of my pockets, I risked another look over my parapet. The silhouette was advancing towards me. It must be one of our men making the rounds, but supposing it was a Bolshevik!

'Grunting with the effort, I pulled my hands from their shelter and grabbed my gun. The breech, sticky with frost, bit into my fingers as I manoeuvred my weapon into firing position and shouted out 'Wer da?' I got back a reasonable reply, and my bullet remained in the gun.

'All the same, I had been prudent to take these elementary precautions; it was an officer doing his rounds. I saluted.

"Everything all right?"

'Yes, Lieutenant.'

'Fine. Well, Happy Christmas.'

'What? Is it Christmas?'

'Yes. Look over there.'

'He pointed to the Khosky's house. The roof, loaded with snow sloped down to ground level; the narrow windows were shining far more brightly than black-out regulations usually permitted, and in their light I could see the swiftly moving silhouettes of my comrades. A few moments later a tall flame burst from an enormous woodpile, which must have been soaked with gasoline.

'A song supported by three-hundred voices ascended slowly into the stillness of the frozen night. 'O Weihnact! O Stille Nacht!' Was it possible? At that moment, everything beyond the perimeter of the camp was without meaning for me. I couldn't tear my eyes from the light of the bonfire. The faces closest to the flames were illuminated; the rest were lost in darkness, while the strong outpouring of song continued, divided now into

55

several parts. Perhaps the circumstances of this particular Christmas night made a critical difference, but in all the time since then I haven't heard anything which moved me so much.

'The memories of my earliest youth, still so close, returned to me for the first time since I had been a soldier. What was happening at home this evening? What was happening in France? We had heard bulletins which informed us that many French troops were now fighting along with us — news which made me rejoice. The thought of Frenchmen and Germans marching side by side seemed marvellous to me. Soon we would no longer have to be cold; the war would be over, and we could all recite our adventures at home. This Christmas hadn't brought me any gift I could hold in my hand, but had brought so much good news about the harmony between my two countries that I felt overwhelmed. Because I knew that I was now a man, I kept firmly at the back of my mind a foolish and embarrassing idea which kept pursuing me: I really would have liked someone to give me an ingenious mechanical toy.

'My companions were still singing, and all along the front millions like them must have been singing as they were. I didn't know that, at that very hour, Soviet T-34 tanks, taking advantage of the truce which Christmas was supposed to bring, were crushing the forward posts of the Sixth Army, in which one of my uncles was serving; men and women were dying by the thousands in the hell of Stalingrad. I didn't know that the German towns were being subjected to the horrifying bombardments of the RAF and the USAF and I would never have dared to think that the French would refuse a Franco-German entente.

'This was, in its way, the most beautiful Christmas I had ever seen, made entirely of disinterested emotion and stripped of all tawdry trimmings. I was all alone beneath an enormous starred sky, and I can remember a tear running down my frozen cheek — a tear neither of pain nor of joy but of emotion created by intense experience.

'By the time I got back to the billet, the officers had put an end to the celebrations, and ordered the bonfire extinguished. Hals had saved a half bottle of schapps for me. I swallowed down a few mouthfuls, not to disappoint him.'

Stan Arneil

No anthology of Australian Christmas would be complete without a quote from Stan Arneil's book, (a war classic incidentally) *One Man's War.*

From his secretly kept diary of his and his mate's time in Changi come the following extracts:

24th December 1942
A very enjoyable battalion dinner tonight on the Padang with the festive spirit abounding. It was a regular reunion after the work parties in Singapore and we hope for a Christmas at home next year.

25th December 1943
Midnight Mass last night by a Dutch, an English and an Aussie priest. The Mass was sung by the Dutchmen present. It was a lovely Mass and Communion made my satisfaction complete. I wonder if Frank went to Midnight Mass?

25th December 1944
Sitting on my bed exuding goodwill in genuine 'after Xmas dinner style.' We are having a far better Xmas

than the previous two as prisoners of war and almost better than the Xmas at Jemaluang. Garry and I went to Midnight Mass last night. It was fairly bright in the open with a half moon and only one candle as allowed by the IJA, the priest's vestments winking here and there in the little chapel made a lovely picture. There were almost a thousand there and all went to Communion. The other chapels were also packed out. Full advantage of the privilege of three Masses per priest was taken and there were Masses galore so I popped over again this morning. Our long saved up feasting is better than we expected. We had extra for breakfast and at lunch Doug and Tommy worked like niggers frying towgay and blachan in oil which they then fried in our rice hash, to make a delicious dish. We had a cup of sweet coffee made on coconut milk for morning tea with a couple of rissoles: the IJA issued every man with six cigars. We had a very jolly tea in the mess and had our supper with the boys. Drunk on food, it doesn't seem possible, but it happened.

It was the best exhibition of universal Xmas spirit I have ever seen. A happy day.

26th December 1944 (Next day. RB)
Together with most of the camp I am visiting the latrines too often for comfort, our stomachs are very upset . . . but it was worth it.

Christmas Carols

Silent Night, Holy Night

What better time to write a Christmas carol than Christmas, and what better church in which to sing it for the first time than the Church of Saint Nicholas in Overndorf, near Salzburg in Austria. The lyricist was the Pastor Joseph Mohr, and the story goes that this shy man attended a pre-Christmas party, on Christmas Eve, at the home of the local schoolmaster, who was also the church organist. After Mohr had shown him the words of the carol he had written, Franz Gruber, the organist, began to hum a tune, and left the room, reading the words of 'Silent Night'. Before he went to sleep that night he had scored the music on a piece of paper, planning to use the new carol and music in church the following morning.

Unfortunately, the next morning, the organ was broken beyond simple and immediate repair, so he hurried home and brought a guitar to the house of worship. At that Christmas morning service on 25 December 1818, Mohr and Gruber sang 'Silent Night' as a duet.

Later, so the story goes, Gruber had to test the organ when the repairs had been completed, and the repairman heard for the first time the tune of 'Silent Night'. They say he was so enchanted that he asked for a copy so that his daughters might include it in their repertoire. A copy was freely given.

Another copy found its way, via the repairman's daughters, to another group in their village of Zillerthall. Four sisters, Strasse by name, took it and presented it at the concerts they gave around the country. It gained its popularity first of all by word of mouth, and, later, when finally published, gained fame as perhaps the most loved of all Christmas carols.

Hark, The Herald Angels Sing
This is another popular carol, by Charles Wesley, who was himself born seven days before Christmas. In all, he wrote and composed some 6500 hymns, but there is little doubt that this is a favourite of all denominations.

Joy to the World
Another prolific hymn writer, Isaac Watts, presented this carol to the Christian Church, and of his 600 hymns this is probably best known.

O Come All Ye Faithful
This well-known Christmas hymn was written by John Francis Wade, an Englishman who lived in France for many years. He wrote the carol in 1744, taking it from an original by Saint Bonaventure written in 1274.

The Boar's Head Carol
This is undoubtedly the oldest of all secular carols, stemming from 1521. The words were written some years before this date, and the tune is supposedly by one Wynkyn de Worde.

The Cherry Tree Carol
Also from the fifteenth century and not quite as ancient as the 'Boar's Head Carol,' this carol's origin is in the legend of the Cherry Tree and Mary.

Some carols and Christmas music

Year of composition	Composer	Title
368	St Hilary	Jesus Light of All the Nations
1250	Thibaud	In Excelsis Gloria!
1274	St Bonaventure	O Come, All Ye Faithful
1400	Traditional	I Saw Three Ships
1521	Traditional	The Boar's Head Carol
1535	Luther	From Heaven Above to Earth I Come
1641	de Brebeuf	Huron Indian Carol
1703	Tate	While Shepherds Watched Their Flocks
1719	Watts	Joy to The World
1739	Wesley	Hark! The Herald Angels Sing
1741	Handel	Messiah
1816	Montgomery	Angels from the Realms of Glory
1818	Mohr	Silent Night! Holy Night!
1825	Bowring	Watchman Tell Us of the Night
1833	Traditional	The First Noel

Year of composition	Composer	Title
1850	Sears	It Came Upon the Midnight Clear
1856	Adams	O Holy Night
1857	Hopkins	We Three Kings of Orient Are
1863	Longfellow	Christmas Bells
1867	Stainer	God Rest You Merry, Gentlemen
1868	Brooks	O Little Town of Bethlehem
1943	Martin and Yon	Gesu Bambino

Prose and Verse

Introduction

Christmas is a time when performers, radio stations and television producers do their research and present the most popular yuletide programmes. The items range from Charles Dickens' *A Christmas Carol,* right down to the ribald doggerel so well-known to soldiers, sailors and, indeed to servicemen all over the world, which begins: 'It was Christmas Day in the . . .', and the venue is changed to suit the situation in which it is recited. Originally, the 'workhouse', but barracks, wardroom, hangar, prison, or what have you, all fit.

Charles Dickens', *A Christmas Carol,* complete with Scrooge, his ghost, Bob Crachit and Tiny Tim, you can find on practically every household bookshelf, but I have chosen some special items, poems and a story for inclusion here. I have taken them from Christmas cards sent to me over the years and various other sources; the poem of Ephraim and *Cranky O'Rielly* are from my own pen.

A Visit From Saint Nicholas

'Twas the night before Christmas, when all through the house
Not a creature was stirring, not even a mouse;
The stockings were hung by the chimneys with care,
In hopes that St Nicholas soon would be there;

The children were nestled all snug in their beds,
While visions of sugar-plums danced in their heads;
And Mamma in her kerchief, and I in my cap,
Had just settled down for a long winter's nap.

When out on the lawn there arose such a clatter,
I sprang from my bed to see what was the matter,
Away to the window I flew like a flash,
Tore open the shutters and threw up the sash.

The moon, on the breast of the new-fallen snow,
Gave a lustre of mid-day to objects below;
When, what to my wandering eyes should appear,
But a miniature sleigh, and eight tiny reindeer,
With a little old driver, so lively and quick,
I knew in a moment it must be St Nick.

More rapid than eagles his coursers they came,
And he whistled and shouted, and called them by name;
'Now Dasher! now, Dancer! now, Prancer and Vixen!
On Comet! on, Cupid! on, Donner and Blitzen!
To the top of the porch, to the top of the wall!
Now, dash away, dash away, dash away, all!'

As dry leaves that before the wild hurricane fly,
When they meet with an obstacle, mount to the sky,
So, up to the house-top the coursers they flew,
With a sleigh full of toys, and St Nicholas, too.

And then in a twinkling, I heard on the roof
The prancing and pawing of each little hoof.
As I drew in my head, and was turning around.
Down the chimney St Nicholas came with a bound.

He was dressed all in fur from head to his foot,
And his clothes were all tarnished with ashes and soot;
His droll little mouth was drawn up like a bow,
And the beard on his chin was as white as the snow.

The stump of a pipe he held tight in his teeth,
And the smoke it encircled his head like a wreath;
A bundle of toys he had flung on his back,
And he looked like a pedlar just opening his pack.

His eyes, how they twinkled! His dimples how merry!
His cheeks were like roses, his nose like a cherry;
He had a broad face and a little round belly
That shook when he laughed, like a bowlful of jelly.

He was chubby and plump, a right jolly old elf;
And I laughed when I saw him, in spite of myself.
A wink of his eye, and a twist of his head.
Soon gave me to know I had nothing to dread.

He spoke not a word, but went straight to his work,
And filled all the stockings; then turned with a jerk
And laying his finger aside of his nose,
And giving a nod, up the chimney he rose.

He sprang to his sleigh, to his team gave a whistle,
And away they all flew like the down of a thistle;
But I heard him exclaim ere he drove out of sight
'Happy Christmas to all, and to all a goodnight!'

Clement C. Moore

Jesus our brother, strong and good
Was humbly born in a stable rude
And the friendly beasts around Him stood
Jesus our brother, strong and good.

'I', said the donkey, shaggy and brown,
'I carried His mother up hill and down;
I carried her safely to Bethlehem town.'
I', said the donkey, shaggy and brown.

'I', said the cow, all white and red,
'I gave Him my manger for His bed
I gave Him my hay to pillow His head,
I', said the cow, all white and red.

'I', said the sheep with the curly horn,
'I gave Him my wool for His blanket warm
He wore my coat on Christmas morn;
I', said the sheep with the crumpled horn.

'I', said the dove from the rafters high
'Cooed Him to sleep, my mate and I
We cooed Him to sleep, my mate and I,
I', said the dove from the rafters high.

And every beast, by some good spell
In the stable dark was glad to tell
Of the gifts he gave Immanuel,
The gift he gave Immanuel.

Author unknown

The mistletoe bough on the festive throng
Looks down, amid echoes of mirthful song
And who is she that will not allow
A kiss claimed under the mistletoe bough

Old English verse

No love that in a family dwells,
No carolling in frosty air,
Not all the steeple shaking bells
Can with this single Truth compare —
That God was Man in Palestine
And lives to-day in Bread and Wine.

Old Christmas verse. Trad.

The door is on the latch to-night,
The hearth fire is aglow;
I seem to hear soft passing feet —
The Christ Child in the snow.

My heart is open wide to-night
For stranger, kith or kin;
I would not bar a single door
Where love might enter in.

Anon.

Christmas Carol

As Joseph was a-wurkin',
He heard an angel sing,
'This night shall be the birth-night
Of Christ our heavenly King.

His birth-bed shall be neither
In housen nor in hall,
Nor in the place of paradise,
But in the oxen's stall.

He neither shall be rocked
In silver nor in gold,
But in the wooden manger
That lieth in the mold.

He neither shall be washen
With white wine nor with red,
But with the fair spring water
That on you shall be shed.

He neither shall be clothed
In purple nor in pall,

But in the fair, white linen
That usen babies all."

As Joseph was a-wurkin',
Thus did the angel sing,
And Mary's Son at midnight
Was born to be our King.

Then be you glad, good people,
At this time of the year;
And light you up your candles,
For His star it shineth clear.

Anon

William Shakespeare makes many references to Christmas:

'Some say that ever 'gainst that season comes wherein our Saviour's birth is celebrated, the bird of dawning singeth all night long: And then, they say, no spirits dare stir abroad; The nights are wholesome; then no planets strike. No fairy takes, no witch has power to charm, so hallowed and so gracious is the time.'

Hamlet

At Christmas I no more desire a rose,
Than wish a snow in May's new-fangled shows.

Love's Labour Lost Act 1 Sc.1

Cranky O'Rielly

Everybody called him Cranky O'Rielly. If you asked where he lived, they would tell you to turn left at the church and follow the dirt road for about eight miles and look for the RMB box bearing his surname.

Mind you, he wasn't always referred to as 'Cranky'. Once upon a time he rejoiced in the name Paddy O'Rielly, but that was when he was younger and first came to the district with his lovely young wife, Kathleen. They had married in Sydney, worked together, and saved the deposit on the place now know as 'Cranky's Farm'.

As a young feller, Paddy worked hard, determined to build both a farm and a life for his bride and family. He sweated and slaved, and Kathleen helped where she could until the inevitable trip to Smalltown hospital where young Terence was born.

Terence became the apple of Paddy's eye, and even though the following years brought four daughters in quick succession, the boy was the focal point of his life.

Paddy and Kathleen took the boy to Smalltown for the baptism. At that time Mass was held in the School of Arts. This didn't suit the passionate young Irishman, so he immediately offered some of the timber from his land as a baptismal gift to build a new church.

So those wonderful years rolled on. Paddy and the boy worked together in the paddocks. And he taught the lad to ride, and ride he could, like a veritable centaur.

The girls Paddy left to Kathleen. He loved and worshipped them, but it was young Terence who claimed his Irish soul.

And every Sunday, come hail or shine, Paddy harnessed the old mare to the buggy and took his family to Mass.

So the halcyon years passed. The boy grew and inherited some of the characteristics of the old man in his love of horses. He, at seventeen or so, would sneak off to Smalltown with the frisky stallion and race him at the local meet. Terence would come home with the smell of drink on his breath, and Paddy would say a few harsh words, but with little effect.

Terence had a mind of his own.

Then one Saturday evening, about seven o'clock, there was a knock on the door. Paddy opened it and there stood the local Sergeant of Police.

Paddy identified his rifle and watched as the policeman took young Terence away. The charge: robbing the local bank. The lad's gambling debts had grown to desperation point.

Ten years' hard labour, the judge said, and Terence went off to serve his time in Sydney's Long Bay Jail.

Paddy went berserk. He blamed the Church and the local priest for lack of guidance and the locals for helping his boy on the road to destruction. He even erased the boy's name from the family Bible.

'He's no son of mine', he would say, 'and what's more, don't ever bring any of them blasted priests here again.'

Broken-hearted Kathleen took it hard. She saved her egg money and every six months went to Sydney to see her beloved son.

Paddy would listen at the door as she reported to the girls all the news of their brother.

But Paddy got worse. He avoided the township, abused the priest when he came, and in general became a thoroughly objectionable character.

He also began to drink.

More often than not he would take the old donkey to the back paddock with the fencing tools in one side of the saddlebag and a bottle of the 'cratur' in the other, returning each evening drunk and disagreeable.

Terence had served seven of his ten years when he was released, and Kathleen brought home the news that the Prison Chaplain had arranged for the boy to go overseas where he might start a new life.

'Good riddance', said Paddy, 'We don't want a race of bank robbers around here.'

So Cranky O'Rielly lived on, making life a hell on earth for all and sundry; rude, desperate and disappointed with a life that held no hope at all.

Not many years after Terence's departure for parts unknown, a new family moved into the adjacent farm.

They had a small son of some seven summers who somehow or other caught Paddy's eye. He even looked like Terence used to look, laughed like him too. He made old Cranky's heart turn over.

Came Christmas, and just before Christmas Eve there was a knock on the door and the unshaven, half-drunk Cranky opened it. It was the lad from next door.

'Excuse me, Mr Cranky,' he started.

Old Cranky blew his top. 'Who told you to call me Cranky?' he yelled.

The lad was frightened but determined. 'All the people call you Cranky O'Rielly,' he said, 'and I thought it was your name.'

'What do you want?' asked Cranky.

'Please sir, Cranky, can I borrow your donkey for Christmas Eve? The new father at the church is having a pageant and I'm 'Joseph'.'

Something in the boy's eyes tugged at Cranky's heart and he said yes. I rather think his tearful eyes made him nod assent.

So it was Christmas Eve.

Kathleen and the girls were ready to go into Smalltown for Midnight Mass and, to their surprise, as they left the house, there was Cranky — sober, for once, shaved for the first time in years, and dressed in his Sunday best with his hat pulled down over his eyes.

The sulky was harnessed and the donkey tied behind. The lad from next door was already sitting up where once Terence sat.

Silently, for fear of breaking the spell, the family climbed aboard and set off for town. Cranky was the quietest of them all.

So to the church, the pageant outside and then on into the sanctuary for Mass. Cranky kept his head down, glaring at the ground and refusing to look at either the townsfolk or the congregation.

And so he sat, and stood, sullenly and silently throughout the whole of the candlelit service.

Then it was his turn.

Still, with head bowed he led his family to the communion rail and knelt. God only knows what thoughts went through his old cranium. He saw the cassock before him and raised his face to receive the Host . . .

And looked straight into the face of the new priest . . . one Father Terence . . .

Who, having served him, placed his hand on the old man's head and said:

'God bless you, Dad, I'll be home with you all for Christmas.'

Ephraim

He was just a scruffy shepherd's boy,
A sort of 'rouseabout'.
He'd gather sticks and tend the fire,
Nor let the lamp blow out.

He'd do those little tedious jobs,
At the shepherds' beck and call;
Too young to be a shepherd yet;
Too old for playing ball.

He rather liked the role he played,
For underneath, he knew,
If he worked hard and learned his trade
He'd be a shepherd true.

And so upon that cold clear night,
When the sky brought forth a star,
He stood with all the older men
And watched it from afar.

Later he heard the angels sing,
And saw them, what is more,
The shepherds let him light their way
Up to the stable door.

'For unto you, this day is born'
He remembered every word,
'A saviour who will be the Christ,
And for you all, "The Lord".'

He worked his hands about his lamp;
He saw the shepherds bow —
Then off they ran to Bethlem's Town,
And Ephraim made his vow.

'I'll take my lamp close by the babe,
And hold it, Him to warm;
The stable's cold — the mother too;
I do not wish him any harm.'

So quietly Ephraim tip-toed in,
To stand behind the stall;
And through the night the lamp burned bright,
Warming the Family all.

Then Mary sweetly smiled at him,
'Thanks, shepherds' boy,' she said;
But Ephraim simply grimaced back,
His arm was made of lead.

And so the morning sun arose,
Its warm rays touched the stall;
Young Ephraim blew and blew his lamp,
But the flame burned straight and tall.

'Ephraim, my son,' a soft voice said,
'Your patient deed's won fame,
Carry the lamp throughout your life;
It will never lose its flame.'

So Ephraim went about the land,
His lamp kept burning still.
For years and years it burned bright,
He did his Father's will.

And when at last his days were done,
He lay by the side of his light;
He heard that self same kindly voice
He had heard on that wondrous night.

'I am the light of the world', it spoke;
'Come find your reward in joy,
For you've kept your faith, and carried my light
From the day when you were a boy.

So Ephraim died, and the lamp flickered out —
His labour of love complete;
Lord make us all lamps, that your light may shine.
As a guide to our wayward feet.

One Solitary Life

Here is a man who was born in an obscure village, the child of a peasant woman. He grew up in another obscure village. He worked in a carpenter's shop until He was thirty, then for three years He was an itinerant preacher. He never wrote a book. He never held an office. He never owned a home. He never set foot inside a big city. He never travelled three-hundred kilometres from the place where He was born. He had no credentials but Himself. He had nothing to do with this world except the naked power of His divine manhood. While still a young man, the tide of popular opinion turned against Him. His friends ran away. One of them denied Him. He was turned over to His enemies. He went through the mockery of a trial. He was nailed upon a cross between two thieves. His executioners gambled for the only piece of his property He had on earth while He was dying, and that was His coat. When He was dead, He was taken down and laid in a borrowed grave through the pity of a friend. Almost twenty centuries have come and gone, and today He is the centrepiece of the human race and the leader of progress. I am far within the mark when I say that all the armies that ever marched, and all the navies that ever sailed, all the air fleets that ever flew, and all the parliaments that ever sat, and all the kings that ever reigned, put together, have not affected the life of a man upon this earth as powerfully as that One Solitary Life.

Yes, Virginia, There is a Santa Claus

Just prior to Christmas in 1897, the then editor of the *New York Sun* received a letter from eight-year-old Virginia O'Hanlon with a strange request. Her letter simply read: 'Papa says, 'if you see it in the *Sun* it is so.' Please tell me the truth. Is there a Santa Claus?'

Here is the immortal reply. It was first published in the *New York Sun* in December 1897. The editor was Frank Church. 'Virginia, your little friends are wrong. They have been affected by the scepticism of a sceptical age. They do not believe except what they see. They think that nothing can be which is not comprehensible by their little minds. All minds, Virginia, whether they be men's or children's, are little. In this great universe of ours, man is a mere insect in intellect as compared with the boundless world about him, as measured by the Intelligence capable of grasping the whole truth.

'Yes, Virginia, there is a Santa Claus. He exists as certainly as love and generosity and devotion exist, and you know that they abound and give your life its highest beauty and joy. Alas! How dreary would be the world if there were not Virginias. There would be no childlike faith then, no poetry, no romance to make tolerable this existence. We should have no enjoyment except in sense and sight. The eternal light with which childhood fills the world would be extinguished.

'Not to believe in Santa Claus! You might as well not believe in fairies!

'You might get your Papa to hire men to watch all the chimneys on Christmas Eve to catch Santa Claus, but even if they did not see Santa Claus coming down, what would that prove? Nobody sees Santa Claus, but that is no sign that there is no Santa Claus. The most real things in the world are those that neither children nor men can see.

'You tear apart a baby's rattle to see what makes the noise inside, but there is a veil covering the unseen world which not the strongest men, nor even the united strength of all the strongest men that ever lived could tear apart. Only faith, fancy, poetry, love, romance, can push aside that curtain and view the supernatural beauty beyond. Is it all real? Ah, Virginia, in all this world there is nothing else real and abiding.

'No Santa Claus? Thank God! he lives, and lives forever. A thousand years from now Virginia, nay, ten thousand years from now, he will continue to make glad the heart of childhood.'

Bibliography

Encyclopedia Brittanica

Vergillus Ferm *Encyclopedia of Religion,* Littlefield and Adams, 1959

Dunkerly *Beyond the Gospels,* Pelican, 1957

The Holy Bible — all versions

Whiston *Josephus: History of the Jews,* Published by William Baynes, 1825

Francis of Assisi, Catholic Publications

Charles Dickens *A Christmas Carol,* Two Shilling Library Edition

Werner Keller *The Bible as History,* Hodder and Stoughton, 1980 edn

Guy Sajer *The Forgotten Soldier,* Harper and Row, 1971

The Christian Calendar, Weidenfeld and Nicolson, 1980

Leach (ed.) *Folklore and Mythology,* Funk and Wagnell, 1975

Jackson *History of the Early Church,* Gollancz, 1940

Arneil, S. *One Man's War,* Alternative Publishing Co-op Ltd, 1981